# Power Maths

# Year 1 Textbook

Series Editor: Tony Staneff

## Ash
Ash is curious.
He likes to
find out about
new things.

flexible

determined

brave

helpful

**Flo**

**Dexter**

**Astrid**

**Sparks**

# Pearson

# Contents

This shows us what page to turn to.

Are you ready to continue our maths journey?

# How to use this book

Do you remember how to use Power Maths?

These pages help us get ready for a new unit.

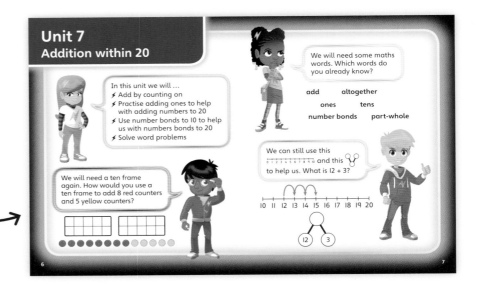

## Discover

Lessons start with Discover.

Have fun exploring new maths problems.

# Share

Next, we share what we found out.

Did we all solve the problems the same way?

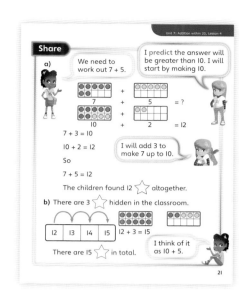

# Think together

Then we have a go at some more problems together.

We will try a challenge too!

This tells you which page to go to in your Practice Book.

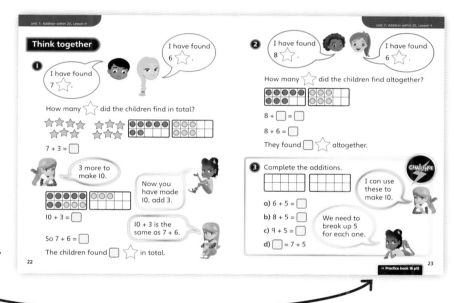

At the end of a unit we will show how much we can do!

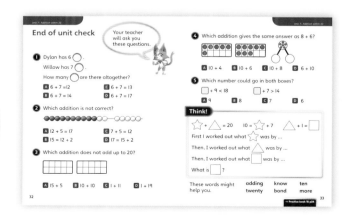

# Unit 7
## Addition within 20

In this unit we will ...
- ⚡ Add by counting on
- ⚡ Practise adding ones to help with adding numbers to 20
- ⚡ Use number bonds to 10 to help us with numbers bonds to 20
- ⚡ Solve word problems

We will need a ten frame again. How would you use a ten frame to add 8 red counters and 5 yellow counters?

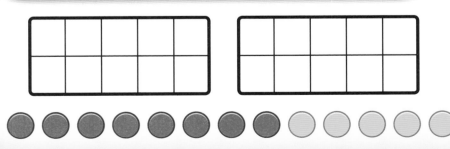

We will need some maths words. Which words do you already know?

**add**     **altogether**

**ones**     **tens**

**number bonds**     **part-whole**

We can still use this

0 1 2 3 4 5 6 7 8 9 10 and this to help us. What is 12 + 3?

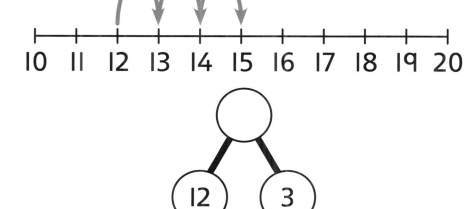

10  11  12  13  14  15  16  17  18  19  20

```
        ( )
       /   \
    (12)   (3)
```

# Add by counting on

**Discover**

**1** **a)** There are 8 children on the  .

There are some children waiting to get on

the  .

How many children are there in total?

**b)** 2 more children arrive to get on the  .

How many children are there in total now?

# Share

**a)**

8 children on the bus and 3 more.

I used ◯ to represent the children.

8 on the bus

9 10 11

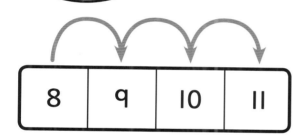

I used a number track to count on 3 more.

8 + 3 = 11

There are 11 children in total.

**b)** 2 more children arrive.

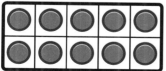 

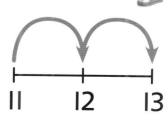

11 + 2 = 13

There are 13 children in total.

# Think together

**1** There are 7 children on the 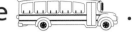 .

5 more children get on the 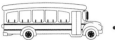 .

How many children are there altogether?

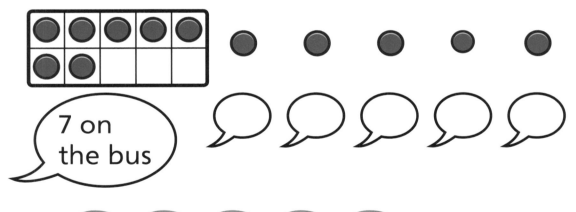

7 on the bus

```
7 + 5 = ☐
```

There are ☐ children altogether.

**2** There are 14 children on the  .

4 more children get on the  .

How many children are there altogether?

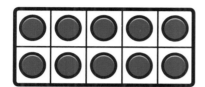 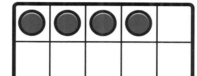

There are ☐ children altogether.

**3** Use the number track to work out these additions.

| 1 | 2 | 3 | 4 | 5 | 6 | 7 | 8 | 9 | 10 | 11 | 12 | 13 | 14 | 15 | 16 | 17 | 18 | 19 | 20 |

**a)** 7 + 2 = ☐

**b)** 4 + 8 = ☐

**c)** 3 + 13 = ☐

Which numbers did you count from?

11

→ Practice book 1B p6

# Adding ones

## Discover

**I** **a)** How many ✂ are there in total?

**b)** How many ✂ would there be if both blocks were full?

## Share

We need to work out 12 + 3.

a)

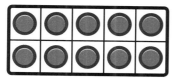

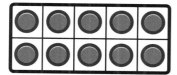

12 is 10 and 2.

2 + 3 = 5.
10 and 5 is 15.

I used a  .

12 + 3 = 15

There are 15  in total.

b)

There are 10 gaps in each block.

10 + 10 = 20

There would be 20 ✂ if both blocks were full.

13

# Think together

**1**

There are 15 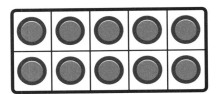 in the tin.

How many 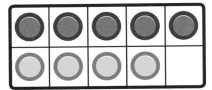 are there altogether?

10 and 5 is ☐.

5 + ☐ = ☐

15 + 4 = ☐

There are ☐ 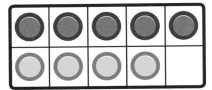 altogether.

**2** There are 13 children in a swimming pool.

4 children dive in.

How many are there now?

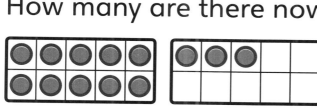

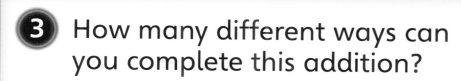

10 and ☐ is ☐ .

3 + ☐ = ☐

13 + ☐ = ☐

There are ☐ children in the pool now.

**3** How many different ways can you complete this addition?

1☐ + ☐ = 18

**CHALLENGE**

 How will this 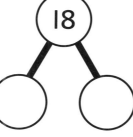 help?

This addition can be completed

_____ different ways.

15

# Finding number bonds

**Discover**

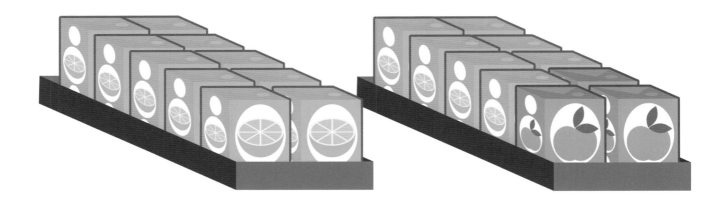

**1** **a)** 3 are apple juice.

How many are orange juice?

**b)**

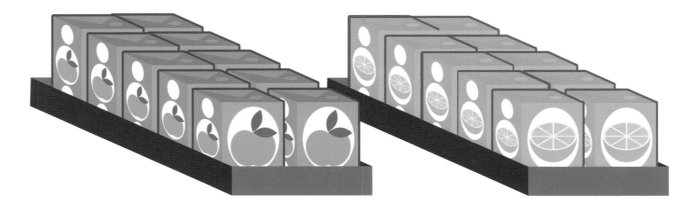

10 are apple juice.

How many are orange juice?

# Share

**a)** I can use a 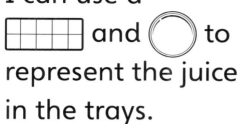 and ◯ to represent the juice in the trays.

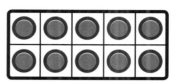 

$7 + 3 = 10$

You can also use a  .

There are 20 juice cartons in total.
I know $7 + 3 = 10$, so I know $17 + 3 = 20$.

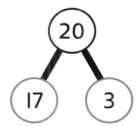

This reminds me of adding the ones in the last lesson.

There are 20  in total.

There are 3 apple  .

$17 + 3 = 20$

17  are orange juice.

**b)**

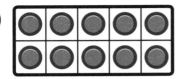  

10  are apple juice.

$10 + 10 = 20$

10  are orange juice.

## Think together

**I**

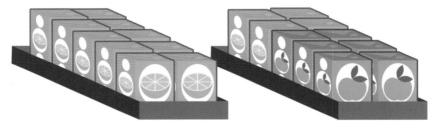

6 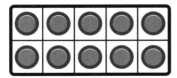 are apple juice.

How many  are orange juice?

$6 + \boxed{\phantom{0}} = 10$

So $6 + \boxed{\phantom{0}} = 20$

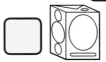 are orange juice.

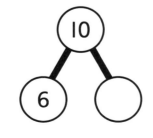 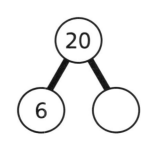

18

**2**

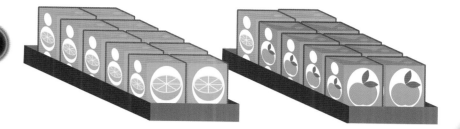

12 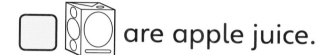 are orange juice.

How many 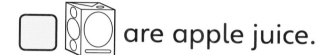 are apple juice?

☐ + ☐ = 20

☐ 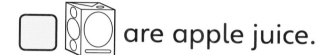 are apple juice.

I used a 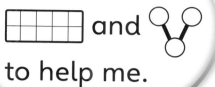 and  to help me.

**3** Complete the number bonds to 20.

1 + ☐ = 20

2 + ☐ = 20

3 + ☐ = 20

11 + ☐ = 20

12 + ☐ = 20

13 + ☐ = 20

☐ + 9 = 20

☐ + 19 = 20

CHALLENGE

How are the bonds linked?

Can you find any other bonds to 20?

19

→ Practice book 1B p12

# Add by making 10 ❶

**Discover**

❶ **a)** How many ☆ have the children found in the classroom altogether?

**b)** There are some ☆ still hidden in the classroom. Find them. What is the total number of ☆?

# Share

a)

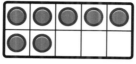 We need to work out 7 + 5.

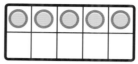 I **predict** the answer will be greater than 10. I will start by making 10.

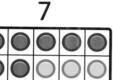 + 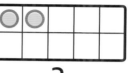 = ?

7 + 5

 + 2 = 12

10

7 + 3 = 10

10 + 2 = 12

So

7 + 5 = 12

 I will add 3 to make 7 up to 10.

The children found 12  altogether.

b) There are 3 ⭐ hidden in the classroom.

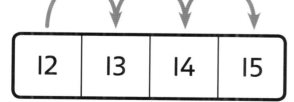

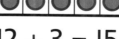

12 + 3 = 15

There are 15 ⭐ in total.

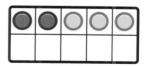 I think of it as 10 + 5.

# Think together

I have found 6 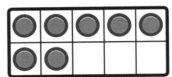 .

**I**

I have found 7  .

How many  did the children find in total?

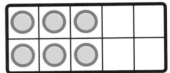

7 + 3 = ☐

3 more to make 10.

Now you have made 10, add 3.

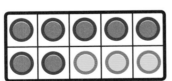

10 + 3 = ☐

10 + 3 is the same as 7 + 6.

So 7 + 6 = ☐

The children found ☐  in total.

**2** 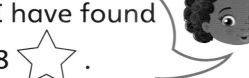 I have found 8  .

I have found 6 ☆ .

How many ☆ did the children find altogether?

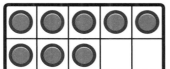

8 + ☐ = ☐

8 + 6 = ☐

They found ☐ ☆ altogether.

**3** Complete the additions.

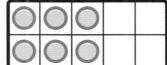

I can use these to make 10.

**a)** 6 + 5 = ☐

**b)** 8 + 5 = ☐

**c)** 9 + 5 = ☐

We need to break up 5 for each one.

**d)** ☐ = 7 + 5

CHALLENGE

23

→ Practice book 1B p15

# Add by making 10 ❷

**Discover**

There are 9 👖 in this box.

**1** **a)** How many 👖 are there in total?

**b)** There are 8 👖 in the box.

Rav finds 4 more 👖.

How many 👖 are there in total?

## Share

a)

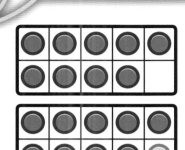 We need to work out 9 + 4.

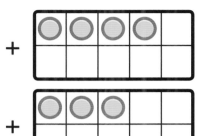 I will use ten frames.

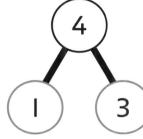

You can also use a number line.

Add 1 to make 10.

Then add the 3.

9  10  11  12  13

$9 + 4 = 13$

There are 13  in total.

b) $8 + 4 = 12$

There are 12  in total.

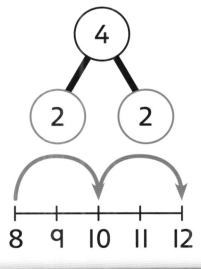

8  9  10  11  12

# Think together

**1**

How many bags are there altogether?

$8 + \boxed{\phantom{0}} = 10$

There are $\boxed{\phantom{0}}$ bags in total.

There are 8 bags in the lost property box.

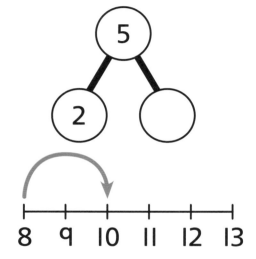

**2**

How many  are there altogether?

$\boxed{\phantom{0}} + \boxed{\phantom{0}} = \boxed{\phantom{0}}$

There are $\boxed{\phantom{0}}$  in total.

There are 6  in the box.

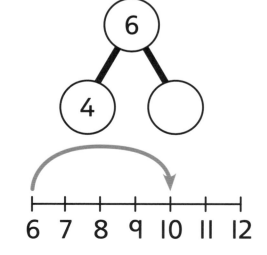

**3** Sam and Jane worked out 5 + 7.

CHALLENGE

I worked out 5 + 7 on a number line.

5  6  7  8  9  10  11  12

I worked out 7 + 5 on a bead string.

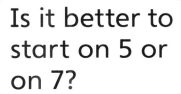

Do they have the same answer?

Is it better to start on 5 or on 7?

27

# Solving word problems – addition

## Discover

**I** **a)** There are 8 yellow  on the shelf.

How many  are on the shelves in total?

**b)** How many  are piled on the floor?

28

## Share

**a)**

I will count on from 8.

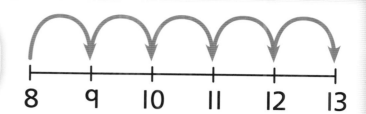
8  9  10  11  12  13

I will add by making 10.

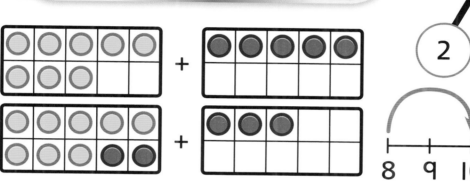 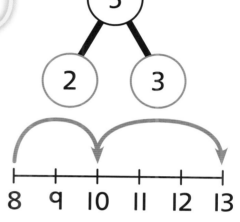

There are 5 red . There are 8 yellow .

5 + 8 = 13

There are 13  on the shelves in total.

**b)**

There are 12 books in one pile.

There are 5 books in the other pile.

2 + 5 = 7

12 + 5 = 17

2 + 5 = 7

There are 17  piled on the floor.

29

# Think together

**1** There are 8 yellow  on the shelf.

The librarian finds 4 more yellow  .

How many yellow  are there in total now?

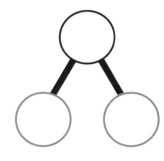

$\boxed{\phantom{0}} + \boxed{\phantom{0}} = \boxed{\phantom{0}}$

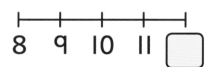

8   9   10   11   $\boxed{\phantom{0}}$

There are $\boxed{\phantom{0}}$ yellow 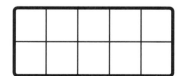 in total now.

**2** How many books has Seth read altogether?

*Last term I read 6 books. This term I have read 11 books.*

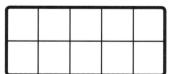

$6 + 1 = \boxed{\phantom{0}}$      $\boxed{\phantom{0}} + \boxed{\phantom{0}} = \boxed{\phantom{0}}$

Seth has read $\boxed{\phantom{0}}$ books altogether.

Seth

**3** Lucy and Seth are reading.

> I know number bonds to 10 and 20.

Each book has 20 pages.

How many pages do they still have to read?

 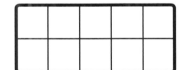

Lucy is on page 12.

$2 + \boxed{\phantom{0}} = 10$

$12 + \boxed{\phantom{0}} = 20$

Lucy has $\boxed{\phantom{0}}$ more pages to read.

Seth is on page $\boxed{\phantom{0}}$.

$\boxed{\phantom{0}} + \boxed{\phantom{0}} = 10$

$\boxed{\phantom{0}} + \boxed{\phantom{0}} = 20$

Seth has $\boxed{\phantom{0}}$ more pages to read.

31

→ Practice book 1B p21

# End of unit check

Your teacher will ask you these questions.

**1** Dylan has 6  .

Willow has 7 ◯ .

How many ◯ are there altogether?

A  6 + 7 = 12

C  6 + 7 = 13

B  6 + 7 = 14

D  6 + 7 = 17

**2** Which addition is not correct?

A  12 + 5 = 17

C  7 + 5 = 12

B  15 = 12 + 2

D  17 = 15 + 2

**3** Which addition does not add up to 20?

A  15 + 5

B  10 + 10

C  1 + 11

D  1 + 19

**4** Which addition gives the same answer as 8 + 6?

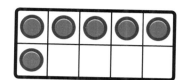 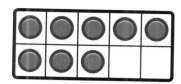 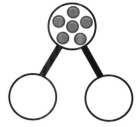

**A** 10 + 4　　　**B** 10 + 6　　　**C** 10 + 8　　　**D** 6 + 10

**5** Which number could go in both boxes?

$\square$ + 9 < 18　　　　　$\square$ + 7 > 14

**A** 9　　　　**B** 8　　　　**C** 7　　　　**D** 6

## Think!

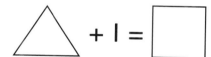

$\bigstar + \triangle = 20$　　　$10 = \bigstar + 7$　　　$\triangle + 1 = \square$

First I worked out what 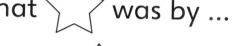 was by ...

Then, I worked out what $\triangle$ was by ...

Then, I worked out what $\square$ was by ...

What is $\square$ ?

These words might help you.　　adding　　know　　ten
　　　　　　　　　　　　　　twenty　　bond　　more

33

→ Practice book 1B p24

# Unit 8
## Subtraction within 20

In this unit we will …
- ⚡ Subtract tens and ones
- ⚡ Learn how to cross a 10 when subtracting
- ⚡ Compare additions and subtractions
- ⚡ Solve word and picture problems

We will need a ten frame again. Can you remember how to use it to help you find the answer to 15 – 3?

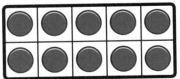

$15 - 3 = \square$

We will need some maths words. Have you seen all of these before?

**subtract**      **take away**

**find the difference**

**how many are left?**

**tens**      **ones**      **number bonds**

**part-whole**

We can also use this
0 1 2 3 4 5 6 7 8 9 10 and this
1 2 3 4 5 6 7 8 9 10 to help us.
What is 13 – 3?

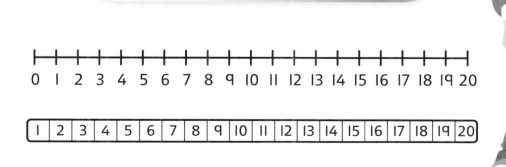

# Subtracting ones

**Discover**

**1** **a)** Mia wants to work out how many  are left.

She works out 15 – 3.

What does the 15 stand for?

What does the 3 stand for?

Why is it a subtraction?

**b)** How many are left?

## Share

**a)** The 15 is the number of  .

The 3 is the number of  being kicked away.

We subtract because we **take away** three  .

**b)**

I will cross out 3  and count how many are left.

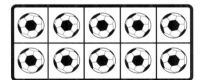 

I can use a ☐☐☐☐☐ and check using a 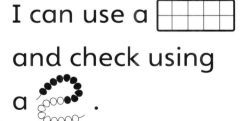 .

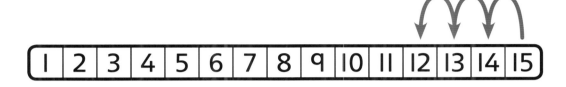

15 − 3 = 12

There are 12  left.

I think it is easier to count back.

37

# Think together

Use 1 ● for each 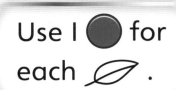.

**1** There are 16  on the tree.

5 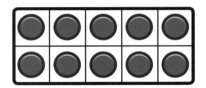 fall to the ground.

How many 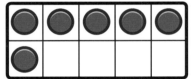 are there left in the tree?

| 1 | 2 | 3 | 4 | 5 | 6 | 7 | 8 | 9 | 10 | 11 | 12 | 13 | 14 | 15 | 16 | 17 | 18 | 19 | 20 |
|---|---|---|---|---|---|---|---|---|---|---|---|---|---|---|---|---|---|---|---|

$16 - 5 = \boxed{\phantom{0}}$

There are $\boxed{\phantom{0}}$  left in the tree.

**2  a)** Work out $19 - 6$.

$19 - 6 = \boxed{\phantom{0}}$

**b)** Work out $16 - 4$.

$16 - 4 = \boxed{\phantom{0}}$

**3** Work out the missing numbers in these number sentences.

CHALLENGE

a)  $7 - 5 = \square$

   $17 - 5 = \square$

I think I can use 7 – 5 to help me answer 17 – 5. I wonder what does not change in 17 – 5.

b)  $8 - 3 = \square$

   $\square - 3 = 15$

c)  $7 - \square = 0$

   $\square - 7 = 10$

When is the answer to a question 0?

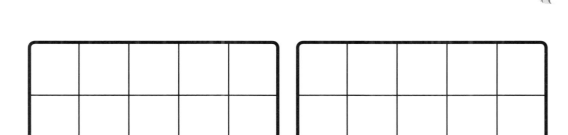

| | | | | | | | | | | | | | | | | | | | |
|---|---|---|---|---|---|---|---|---|---|---|---|---|---|---|---|---|---|---|---|
| 1 | 2 | 3 | 4 | 5 | 6 | 7 | 8 | 9 | 10 | 11 | 12 | 13 | 14 | 15 | 16 | 17 | 18 | 19 | 20 |

39

# Subtracting tens and ones

**Discover**

**1** **a)** There are 15  .

How many have eggs?

How many do not have eggs?

**b)** 13 dive into the sea.

How many are left on the ice?

# Share

**a)**

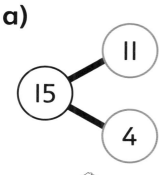

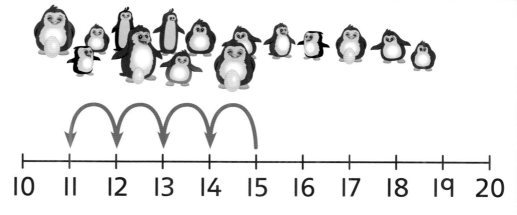

10  11  12  13  14  15  16  17  18  19  20

4  have eggs.

15 – 4 = 11

11  do not have eggs.

**b)** 13  dive into the sea.

I can count back 13 from 15. This takes time and I often make mistakes.

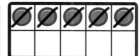

15 – 10 = 5

 5 –  3 = 2

So

15 – 13 = 2

There are 2  left on the ice.

I know that 13 is 10 and 3. I can subtract the 10 first and then 3.

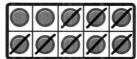

41

# Think together

1

There are 18 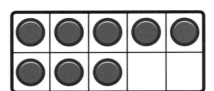 .

A penguin eats 12 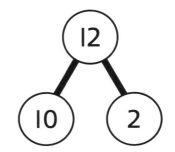 .

How many are left?

Use 1 ⬤ for each  .

18 − 10 = ☐

☐ − 2 = ☐

So

18 − 12 = ☐

There are ☐ 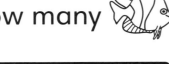 left.

**2** Work out 19 − 14.

19 − ☐ = ☐

☐ − ☐ = ☐

So

19 − 14 = ☐

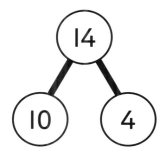

**3** What is 18 − 15?

I subtracted 10 first and then 5.

Danny

I subtracted 5 first and then 10.

Tamsin

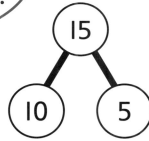

Do Danny and Tamsin get the same answer?

Danny

18 − 10 = ☐

☐ − ☐ = ☐

So

18 − 15 = ☐

Tamsin

18 − 5 = ☐

☐ − ☐ = ☐

So

18 − 15 = ☐

**CHALLENGE**

43

→ Practice book 1B p29

# Subtraction – crossing the 10 ①

**Discover**

① **a)** How many players are there altogether?

How many players are injured?

How many players are not injured?

**b)** There are 15 🍼 of water.

9 players drink one 🍼 each.

How many 🍼 are there left?

# Share

**a)**

There are 11 players.

4 players are injured.

$$11 - 4 = 7$$

There are 7 players not injured.

**b)**

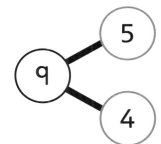

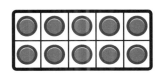
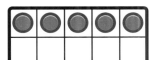

$$15 - 5 = 10$$

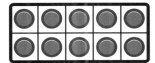
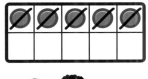

$$10 - 4 = 6$$

We can break 9 into two parts. We subtract 5 first, then 4.

$$15 - 5 = 10$$
$$10 - 4 = 6$$
So
$$15 - 9 = 6$$

There are 6  left.

Why did we subtract 5 first?

# Think together

**1** There are 12 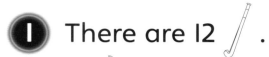 .

7  break.

How many  do not break?

12 − ⬚ = 10

10 − ⬚ = ⬚

So

12 − 7 = ⬚

⬚ 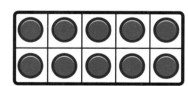 do not break.

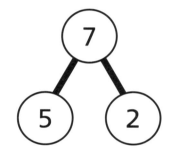

**2** Work out 16 − 9.

16 − ⬚ = ⬚

⬚ − ⬚ = ⬚

So

16 − 9 = ⬚

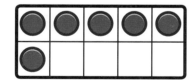

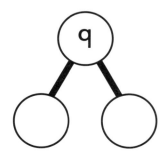

**3** Which 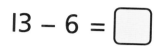 would you use for which question?

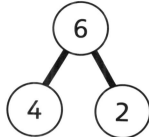

$13 - 6 = \boxed{\phantom{0}}$

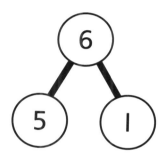

$12 - 6 = \boxed{\phantom{0}}$

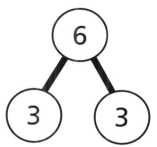

$15 - 6 = \boxed{\phantom{0}}$

CHALLENGE

I think to do 15 – 6 I first subtract 3. Then I subtract another 3.

I am not sure that is the best way of doing it.

47

→ Practice book 1B p32

# Subtraction– crossing the 10 ②

**Discover**

**1 a)** How many ✏ are there?

How many children need a ✏?

How many ✏ are left?

**b)** Show your calculation on a 0 1 2 3 4 5 6 7 8 9 10 or

1 2 3 4 5 6 7 8 9 10 .

# Share

a) There are 13 .

5 children need a .

13 − 5 = ☐

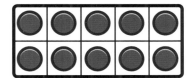 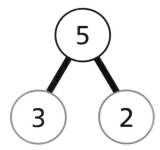

> I can break 5 into two parts.
> I then subtract each part.

13 − ③ = 10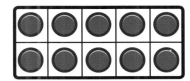

10 − ② = 8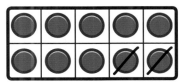

13 − 3 = 10
10 − 2 = 8

So

13 − 5 = 8

There are 8 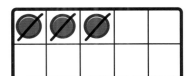 left.

**b)**

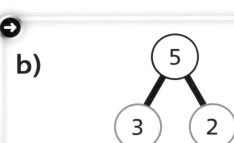

I will use a  0 1 2 3 4 5 6 7 8 9 10 .
I always try to jump to 10, so I will jump back 3 all in one go.

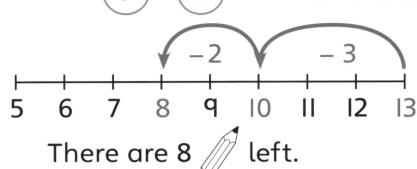

$13 - 3 = 10$

$10 - 2 = 8$

So

$13 - 5 = 8$

There are 8 left.

## Think together

**1** The teacher has 16 ▱ .

7 children need a ▱ .

How many ▱ are there left?

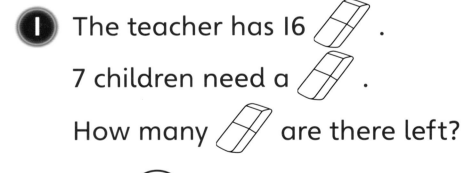

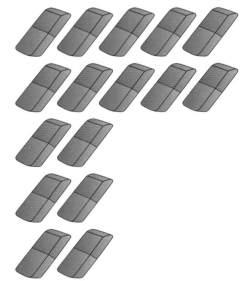

$16 - \boxed{\phantom{0}} = 10$

$10 - \boxed{\phantom{0}} = \boxed{\phantom{0}}$

So

$16 - 7 = \boxed{\phantom{0}}$

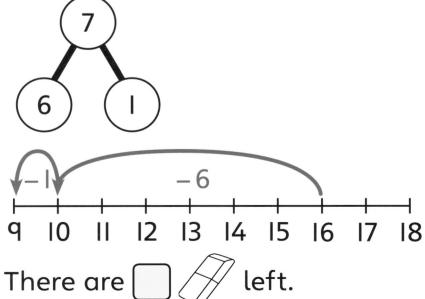

There are ☐ ▱ left.

**2** There are 15 boys in the class.

There are 8 girls in the class.

How many more boys are there than girls?

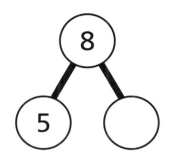

$\boxed{\phantom{0}} - \boxed{\phantom{0}} = \boxed{\phantom{0}}$

$\boxed{\phantom{0}} - \boxed{\phantom{0}} = \boxed{\phantom{0}}$

So

$15 - 8 = \boxed{\phantom{0}}$

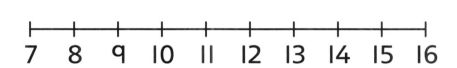

There are $\boxed{\phantom{0}}$ more boys than girls.

---

**3** Work out these subtractions.

a) $20 - 12 = \boxed{\phantom{0}}$

b) $20 - \boxed{\phantom{0}} = 9$

→ **Practice book 1B p35**

# Solving word and picture problems – subtraction

**Discover**

Ray

**1** **a)** The tower is made from 17 blocks.

Ray takes 6 blocks from the tower.

How many blocks are left?

**b)** How many more spotty blocks than plain blocks are there in the castle?

**Share**

I can work this out in different ways.

a)

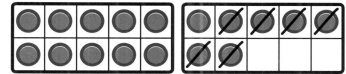

| 1 | 2 | 3 | 4 | 5 | 6 | 7 | 8 | 9 | 10 | 11 | 12 | 13 | 14 | 15 | 16 | 17 |

$17 - 6 = 11$

There are 11 blocks left.

b) The castle has 19 blocks.

There are 14 spotty blocks.

There are 5 plain blocks.

I will line the blocks up. First I subtract 4, then I subtract 1.

$14 - 4 = 10$

$10 - 1 = 9$

So

$14 - 5 = 9$

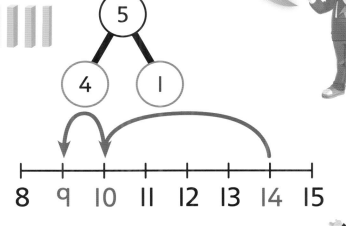

There are 9 more spotty blocks than plain blocks in the castle.

I used a [number line] to help me.

53

# Think together

**1** Pete builds a tower.

7 blocks are knocked off.

How many blocks are left in the tower?

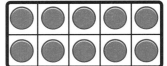 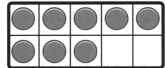

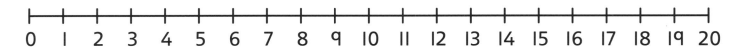

0  1  2  3  4  5  6  7  8  9  10  11  12  13  14  15  16  17  18  19  20

18 − 7 = ☐

There are ☐ blocks left in the tower.

**2** How many more spotty blocks than plain blocks are in Pete's tower?

☐ − ☐ = ☐

☐ − ☐ = ☐

So

☐ − ☐ = ☐

There are ☐ more spotty blocks than plain blocks.

**3**

CHALLENGE

Match the question to the number sentence.

| How many white tiles are there? |

| 16 – 4 |

| How many fewer black tiles are there than white tiles? |

| 16 – 7 |

| 7 tiles crack. How many tiles are not cracked? |

| 12 – 4 |

I wonder what each number represents?

→ **Practice book 1B p38**

# Addition and subtraction facts to 20

**Discover**

**1** **a)** How many fingers are the children holding up?

☐ + ☐ = ☐

**b)** Work out the missing numbers.

13 + ☐ = 20        5 + ☐ = 20

☐ + 13 = 20        20 − 5 = ☐

## Share

**a)** Ray holds up 8 fingers.

Tamsin holds up 10 fingers.

8 + 10 = 18 or 10 + 8 = 18

The children are holding up 18 fingers.

**b)**

 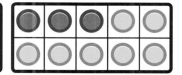

 I can show this using a  .

13 + 7 = 20

7 + 13 = 20

I know that 13 + 7 = 20. This means I also know that 7 + 13 = 20. I know that these are from the same fact family.

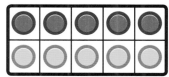 

5 + 15 = 20

20 − 5 = 15

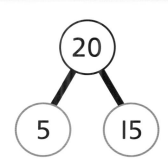

## Think together

**1** There are 20 counters in a box.

12 of the counters are red. The rest are yellow.

How many yellow counters are in the box?

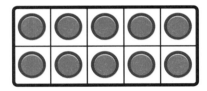 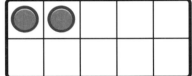 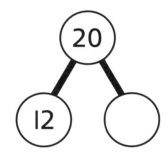

12 + ☐ = 20

There are ☐ yellow counters in the box.

**2** Complete the **fact family**.

a)

19 + ☐ = 20

☐ + 19 = 20

20 – ☐ = ☐

20 – ☐ = ☐

b)

14 + ☐ = 20

☐ + ☐ = 20

☐ – ☐ = ☐

☐ – ☐ = ☐

**3**

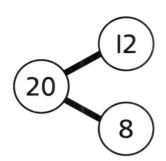

**a)** Show this  using 2 ▭▭ or a 🔗 .

**b)** Complete the fact family.

☐ + ☐ = ☐          ☐ − ☐ = ☐

☐ + ☐ = ☐          ☐ − ☐ = ☐

I can work out eight facts.

I thought there were only four.

→ **Practice book 1B p41**

# Comparing additions and subtractions

## Discover

1  a) Which child is correct?

b) Whose answer is greater, Ben's or Jacob's?

## Share

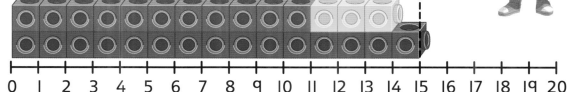
I can make each calculation with cubes.

**a)**

Gita

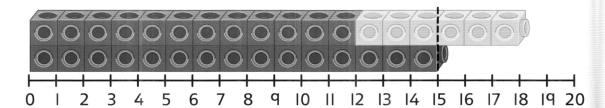

11 + 3

11 + 3 = 14

14 < 15

11 + 3 < 15

Jacob

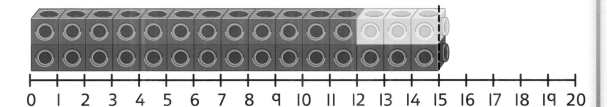

12 + 6

12 + 6 = 18

18 > 15

12 + 6 > 15

Ben

12 + 3

12 + 3 = 15

Jacob is correct.

**b)**

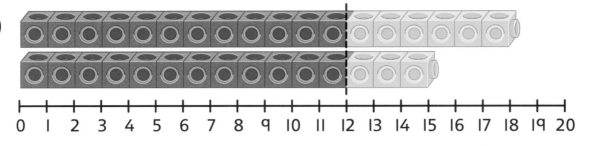

12 + 6 > 12 + 3

Jacob's answer is greater than Ben's answer.

I do not need to work out the answers. 12 is the same. I only need to look at the 6 and 3.

# Think together

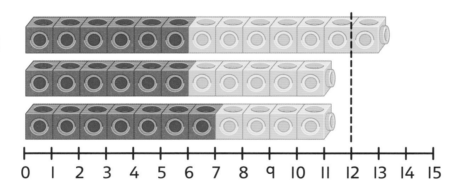

Complete using <, > or =.

6 + 7 ◯ 12

6 + 7 ◯ 6 + 5

6 + 5 ◯ 7 + 4

**2** Who has the greater answer?

 Gita

$11 + 3$

 Ben

$12 + 3$

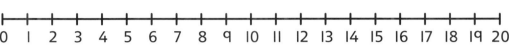

$11 + 3$ ◯ $12 + 3$

_____ has the greater answer.

**3**

Em

$9 +$ [ ]

Well done. You have an answer greater than 15.

CHALLENGE

What number could Em's hand be over?

How many answers can you find?

$9 +$ [ ] $> 15$

I am going to try numbers in order.

# Solving word and picture problems – addition and subtraction

**Discover**

**1** **a)** How many are there in total?

**b)** There are 19 🐌 inside the log.

How many more 🐌 are there inside the log than on the log?

## Share

**a)** There are 8 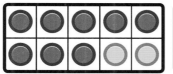 carrying a leaf.

There are 4 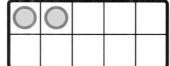 not carrying a leaf.

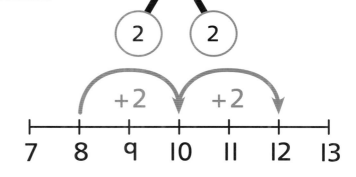

$8 + 2 = 10$

$10 + 2 = 12$

So

$8 + 4 = 12$

There are 12 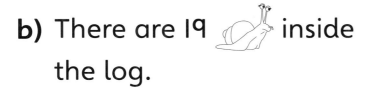 in total.

**b)** There are 19 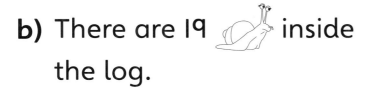 inside the log.

There are 6 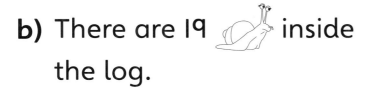 on the log.

$19 - 6 = 13$

There are 13 more 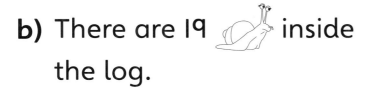 inside the log than on the log.

To work out how many more we must find the difference. This is a subtraction.

# Think together

**1** There are 14 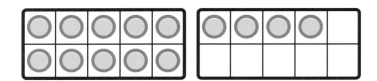 in a hive. 6 🐝 fly away.

How many 🐝 are there left in the hive?

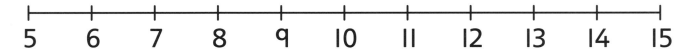

$14 - \boxed{\phantom{0}} = 10$

$10 - \boxed{\phantom{0}} = \boxed{\phantom{0}}$

So

$14 - 6 = \boxed{\phantom{0}}$

There are $\boxed{\phantom{0}}$ bees left in the hive.

**2** How many spots are there altogether?

$\boxed{\phantom{0}} + \boxed{\phantom{0}} = 10$

$\boxed{\phantom{0}} + \boxed{\phantom{0}} = \boxed{\phantom{0}}$

So

$\boxed{\phantom{0}} + \boxed{\phantom{0}} = \boxed{\phantom{0}}$

There are $\boxed{\phantom{0}}$ spots altogether.

**3**

There are 17 stars in the box.

**a)** 12 ☆ are removed. How many ☆ are left in the box?

There are ☐ ☆ left in the box.

**b)** 12 ☆ are gold. The rest are silver.

How many silver ☆ are there?

There are ☐ silver ☆ .

**c)** There are also 12 ⬭ in the box.

How many more ☆ than ⬭ are there?

There are ☐ more ☆ than ⬭ .

**d)** What is the same about the questions and answers?

→ Practice book 1B p47

# End of unit check

Your teacher will ask you these questions.

**1** $16 - 4 = \boxed{\phantom{0}}$

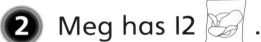

**A** 20 **B** 13 **C** 2 **D** 12

**2** Meg has 12 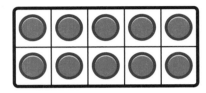.

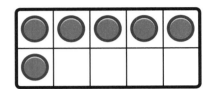

She gives 7  away.

How many 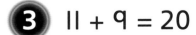 does she have left?

**A** 5 **B** 6 **C** 19 **D** 10

**3** $11 + 9 = 20$

Which of these facts is **not** correct?

**A** $9 + 11 = 20$ **C** $11 - 20 = 9$

**B** $20 - 9 = 11$ **D** $20 = 11 + 9$

**4** What symbol should go in the circle to make the number sentence correct?

12 + 7 ◯ 12 + 5

**A** >          **B** <          **C** =          **D** none of these

**5** Find the missing number

13 − ☐ = 6

**A** 19          **B** 7          **C** 6          **D** 8

## Think!

Molly is subtracting numbers from 10 and 20.

I will subtract 6 first. Then I will subtract 2.

10 − 6 = 4

20 − 6 = 14

10 − 2 = 8

20 − 2 = 18

What do you notice?

Is this always the case for any number from 0 to 10?

These words might help you.

more        less

ten        subtract

→ Practice book 1B p50

# Unit 9
## Numbers to 50

In this unit we will ...
- ⚡ Count up to 50
- ⚡ Compare numbers to 50
- ⚡ Order numbers
- ⚡ Count in 2s and 5s
- ⚡ Solve word and picture problems

We can use a number line to help us order and compare numbers. Which number is larger, 12 or 21?

We will need some maths words and signs.
Do you remember these?

**tens**          **ones**

   **compare**      **order**

**less than (<)**      **greater than (>)**

We can use different things to show the value of a number. We can use ▭▭▭▭▭ , 〰️ or ▭▭▭ . What number is shown here?

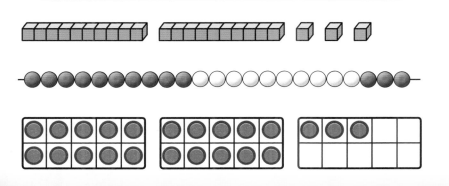

# Counting to 50 ①

## Discover

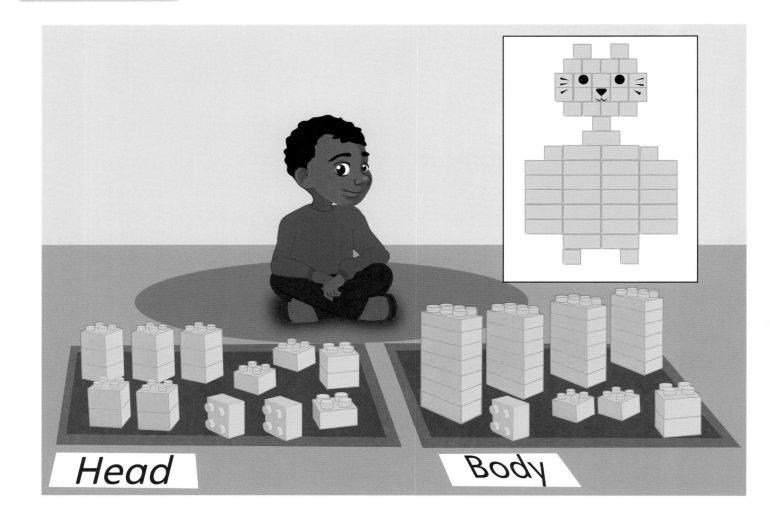

Head

Body

① **a)** Count the bricks needed for the cat's body.

How did you count them?

**b)** Count all the bricks needed to make the cat.

# Share

**a)**

> After every 9, I need to make a new 10. Then after I make a 10, I count from 1 again.

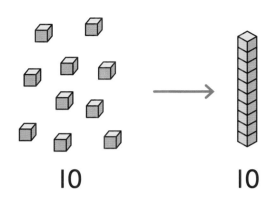

10 → 10

> What is after 29? Is it twenty ten?

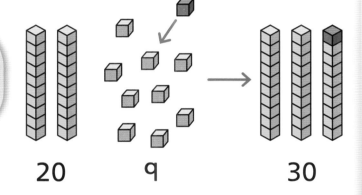

20      9      30

You need 30 bricks to make the cat's body.

**b)**

| 31 | 32 | 33 | 34 | 35 | 36 | 37 | 38 | 39 | 40 |
|---|---|---|---|---|---|---|---|---|---|
| thirty-one | thirty-two | thirty-three | thirty-four | thirty-five | thirty-six | thirty-seven | thirty-eight | thirty-nine | forty |

| 41 | 42 | 43 | 44 | 45 | 46 | 47 | 48 | 49 | 50 |
|---|---|---|---|---|---|---|---|---|---|
| forty-one | forty-two | forty-three | forty-four | forty-five | forty-six | forty-seven | forty-eight | forty-nine | fifty |

You need 50 bricks to make the cat.

# Think together

**1** Fill in the missing numbers.

| 40 | | 42 | 43 | |

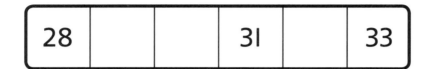

| 28 | | | 31 | | 33 |

**2** What are the missing numbers in the number line and the number track?

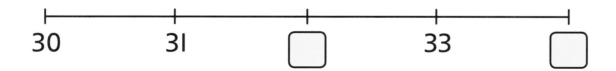

30    31    ☐    33    ☐

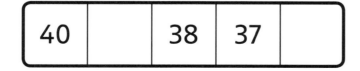

| 40 | | 38 | 37 | |

There are 50  in the jar.

Take one out.

How many are there now?

Take one more out.

How many are there now?

I will count back from 50.

→ Practice book 1B p52

# Counting to 50 ②

**Discover**

**1** **a)** Which number is the lily pad on?

How do you know?

**b)** The  jumps back to the pond.

What numbers does the jump over?

# Share

a)

The lily pad is on number 32.

I counted backwards.

b)

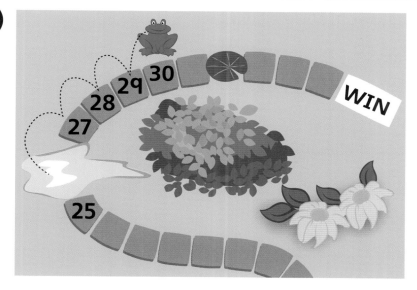 

The jumps back over 3 numbers, 29, 28 and 27, to get to the pond.

# Think together

**1** Which numbers does the 🐸 jump over to get to the pond?

| 21 | 22 | 23 | 24 | 25 | 26 | 27 | 28 | 29 | 30 |
|----|----|----|----|----|----|----|----|----|----|
| 31 | 🐸 | 33 | 34 | 35 | 36 | | 38 | 39 | 40 |

**2** What are the missing numbers?

**a)**

| 1 | 2 | 3 | 4 | 5 | 6 | 7 | 8 | 9 | 10 |
|----|----|----|----|----|----|----|----|----|----|
| 11 | 12 | 13 | 14 | 15 | | 17 | 18 | 19 | 20 |
| 21 | | 23 | 24 | 25 | 26 | 27 | 28 | 29 | 30 |
| 31 | 32 | 33 | 34 | 35 | 36 | 37 | 38 | 39 | |
| 41 | 42 | | 44 | 45 | 46 | 47 | 48 | 49 | 50 |

**b)**

| 14 | 15 | 16 | | 18 |
|----|----|----|----|----|

| 21 | 22 | | 24 | 25 |
|----|----|----|----|----|

| 37 | | 39 | 40 | | 42 | 43 | 44 | 45 |
|----|----|----|----|----|----|----|----|----|

**CHALLENGE**

**3** Ben is lost in the forest.

He must find his way from 34 to 45, in order.

Can you help him to find his way out?

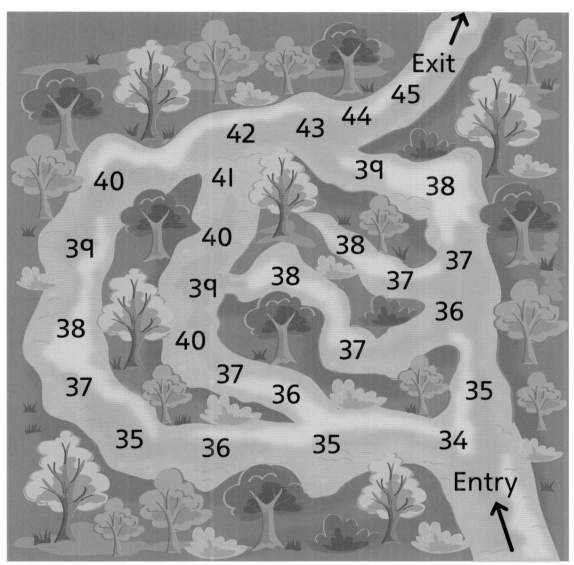

How did you help him find the way?

79

# Tens and ones

**Discover**

Eggs for sale

**1  a)** How many are there in total?

   **b)** A box holds 10 .

   How many full boxes can you make?

# Share

**a)**

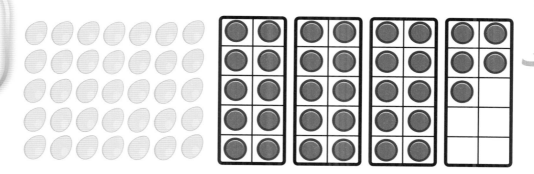

I counted the  one at a time.

Use I ◯ for each 🥚.

There are 35 🥚 in total.

I used each ▭ to show a complete box of eggs.

**b)**

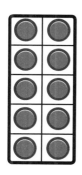 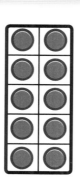 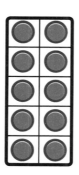 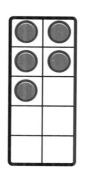

35 is 3 tens and 5 ones.

There are 3 full boxes.

# Think together

**1** How many  are there in total?

There are ☐ 🥚 in total.

☐ is ☐ tens and ☐ ones.

**2** Write the numbers that the counters show.

a)

☐ tens and ☐ ones is ☐ .

b)

☐ tens and ☐ ones is ☐ .

c)

☐ tens and ☐ ones is ☐ .

**3** Look at the table below for the number 28.

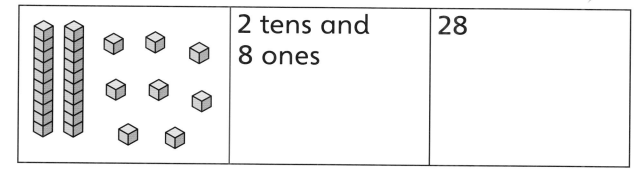

| | 2 tens and 8 ones | 28 |
|---|---|---|

Make your own table for the number 34.

83

→ Practice book 1B p58

# Representing numbers to 50

## Discover

**1 a)** How many different ways can you show 34?

Use the objects on the table.

**b)** Complete the sentences to show how 34 is made.

34 = ☐ tens ☐ ones

34 = 30 and ☐

## Share

You first need to find out how many tens and how many ones there are.

I used beads to show 34.

**a)**

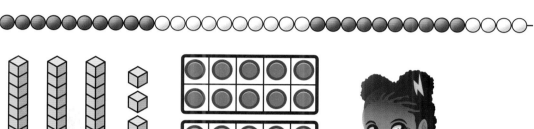

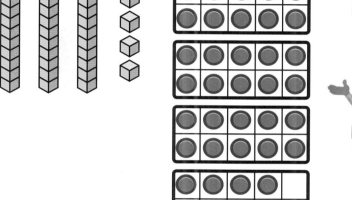

I used ☐ to show 34.

**b)**

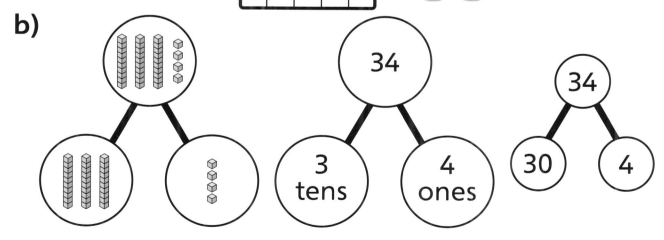

34 = 3 tens 4 ones

34 = 30 and 4

# Think together

**1** Copy and complete each 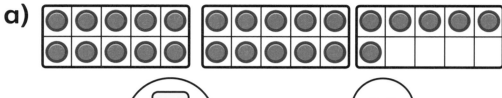.

a)

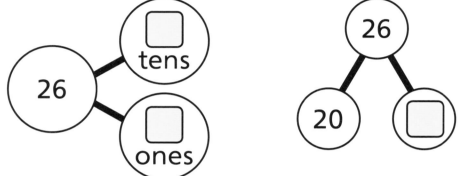

b)

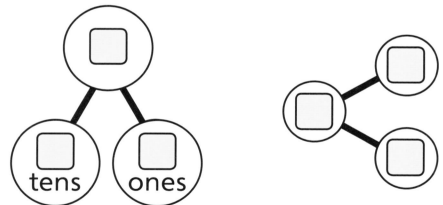

**2** Show this 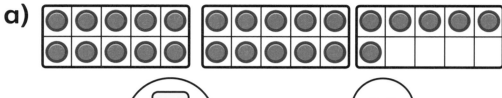 using different objects.

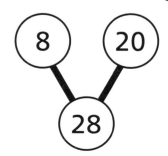

How many different objects can you use?

**CHALLENGE**

**3**

Filip        Molly

Filip and Molly are making numbers.
Filip is making the tens.
Molly is making the ones.
Choose the number they make each time.

4 tens

24

42

2 ones

20

22

I have one.        I have three.

13

31

→ **Practice book 1B p61**

# Comparing numbers of objects

**Discover**

**1** **a)** Who has more ⬭? Eve or Kasim?

How do you know?

**b)** Who has more ⬭? Joe or Kasim?

▢ > ▢

# Share

**a)**

I counted all of the .

I compared the ◯.

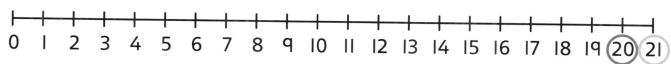

0  1  2  3  4  5  6  7  8  9  10  11  12  13  14  15  16  17  18  19  ⟨20⟩ ⟨21⟩

Kasim has more ◯ than Eve.

21 is greater than 20.

**b)**

19  20 ⟨21⟩ 22  23  24 ⟨25⟩ 26  27

Joe has more ◯.

25 > 21

Counting on from 1, I first meet 21, then 25, so 25 is greater than 21.

# Think together

1   Look at the  and compare the amounts using < or >.

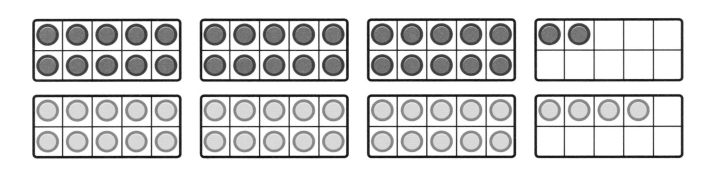

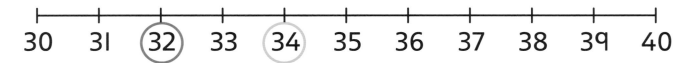

**2** Use a number line to compare the .

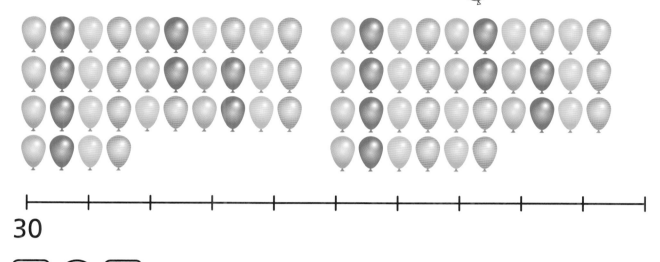

30

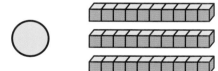

**3** Complete each number sentence.

CHALLENGE

a)

b)

c)  <  [ ]

→ Practice book 1B p64

# Comparing numbers

**Discover**

**RESULTS**

**Ola**
28 star jumps
27 sit-ups

**Ben**
32 star jumps
24 sit-ups

Ola

Ben

**1** **a)** Who has done more star jumps?

**b)** Who has done more sit-ups?

**Share**

I can see that Ben has more tens.

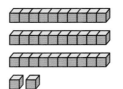

**a)**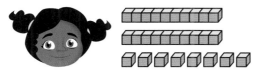

32 > 28

22  23  24  25  26  27  (28)  29  30  31  (32)  33  34

Ben has done more star jumps.

**b)**

They have the same number of tens.
I think I need to compare the ones.

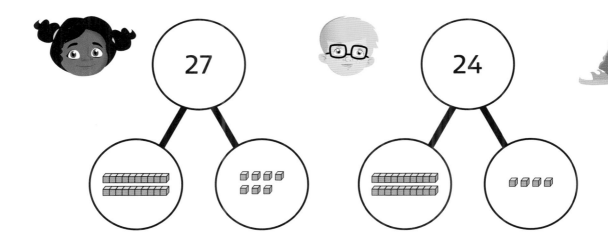

27   24

27 > 24

Ola has done more sit-ups.

# Think together

Anya
40 press-ups

Chen
35 press-ups

**1** Anya   Chen

## Who has done more press-ups?

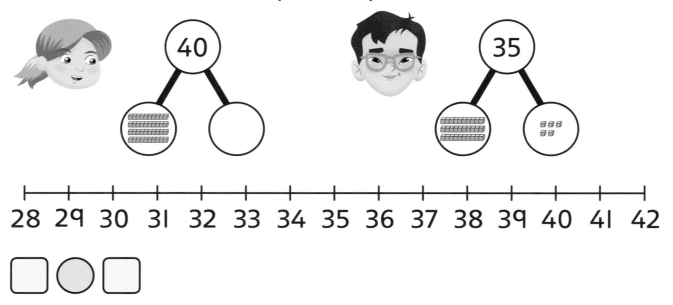

| 28 | 29 | 30 | 31 | 32 | 33 | 34 | 35 | 36 | 37 | 38 | 39 | 40 | 41 | 42 |

☐ ◯ ☐

_____ has done more press-ups.

**2** Write all the numbers that could be used to complete each number sentence.

a)

☐ > 34

| 30 | 39 | 34 |
| 35 | 31 | 33 | 38 |

b)

☐ < 49

| 42 | 40 | 46 |
| 45 | 43 | 48 |

**3** Who swam more lengths?

Gita

Charles

45 lengths
Gita

41 lengths
Charles

35

Try to think of all these numbers on a number line.

□ ○ □

_____ swam more lengths.

95

# Ordering objects and numbers

**Discover**

**1** **a)** Which colour leaves appear the least?

Which colour leaves appear the most?

**b)** Order the number of leaves of each colour.

Start with the smallest.

**Share**

I counted each group in turn.

a)

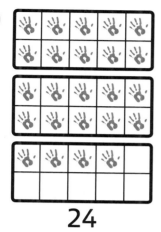

24

12

26

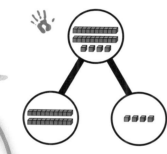

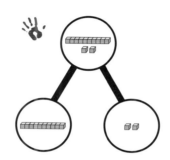

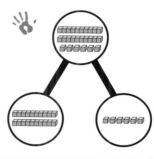

I will look at the tens first. Blue has fewest leaves as it has less tens than the other numbers.

The other numbers have the same number of tens. I need to compare the ones.

The blue leaves appear the least.

The brown leaves appear the most.

b)

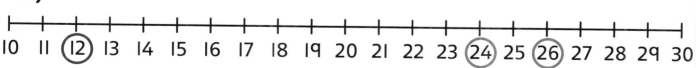

10  11  (12)  13  14  15  16  17  18  19  20  21  22  23  (24)  25  (26)  27  28  29  30

[12] ( < ) [24] ( < ) [26]

# Think together

**1**

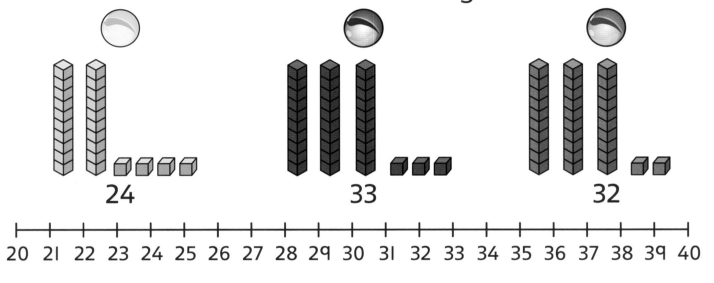

Put the amounts in order starting with the smallest.

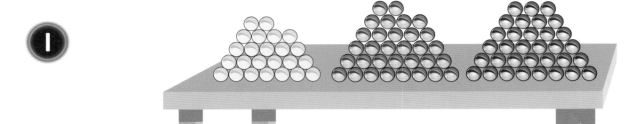

24          33          32

| 20 | 21 | 22 | 23 | 24 | 25 | 26 | 27 | 28 | 29 | 30 | 31 | 32 | 33 | 34 | 35 | 36 | 37 | 38 | 39 | 40 |

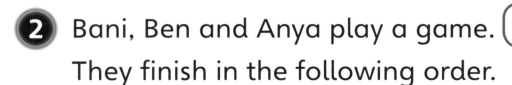

**2** Bani, Ben and Anya play a game.
They finish in the following order.

Their scores were 39, 45, and 40.
Who scored each score?

| 30 | 31 | 32 | 33 | 34 | 35 | 36 | 37 | 38 | 39 | 40 | 41 | 42 | 43 | 44 | 45 | 46 | 47 | 48 | 49 | 50 |

**3** **a)** Put the following number cards in order. Start with the smallest.

**CHALLENGE**

| 35 | 25 | 41 | 27 |

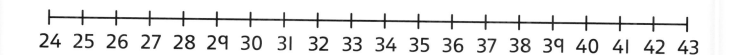

24  25  26  27  28  29  30  31  32  33  34  35  36  37  38  39  40  41  42  43

I could use ▭▭▭▭ or ◯ and a ▭▭ to help me.

**b)** Here are 4 more cards.

| 17 | 28 | 25 | |

28 > 25 > ☐ > 17

What could the blank card be?

I wonder if there is more than one answer?

99

# Counting in 2s

**Discover**

**1** **a)** There are 5 bikes.

How many  are there?

**b)** 2 more bikes cross the finish line.

How many  are there now?

# Share

I counted the 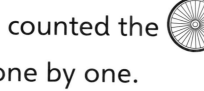 one by one.

**a)**

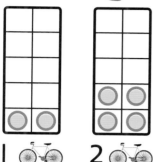 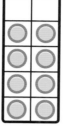 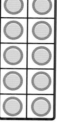

1 2 3 4 5

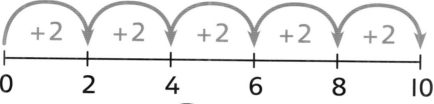

+2  +2  +2  +2  +2

0    2    4    6    8    10

There are 10  .

I counted in 2s.

**b)**

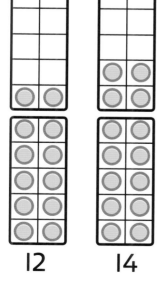

12          14

+2      +2

10      12      14

There are 14  now.

# Think together

**1** There are 12 pairs of shoes.

How many shoes are there in total?

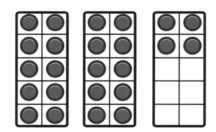

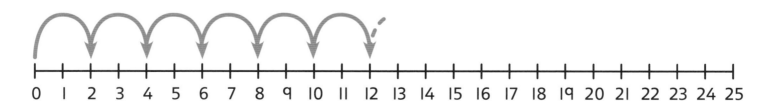

There are ☐ shoes in total.

**2** There are 16 shoes. How many pairs are there?

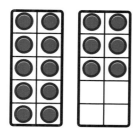

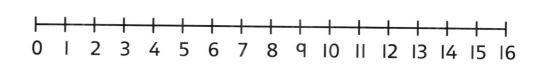

There are ☐ pairs of shoes.

**CHALLENGE**

**3** Complete each number track.

a)

| 16 | 18 |  | 22 |  | 26 | 28 |  | 32 |

b)

|  | 30 | 32 |  |  | 38 |  | 42 |  |

c)

| 40 |  |  | 34 | 32 |  | 28 |

I can see all these numbers
end in 0, 2, 4, 6 or 8.
Is this always true?

→ **Practice book 1B p73**

# Counting in 5s

**Discover**

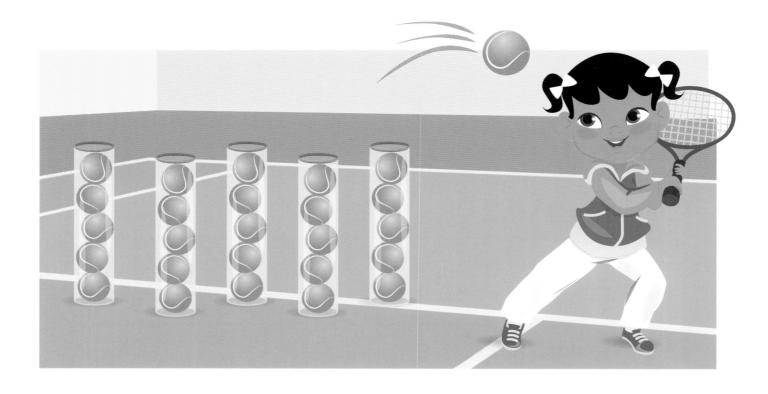

**1** **a)** How many ⬤ are there in 5 tubes?

**b)** How many ⬤ are there in 6 tubes?

# Share

**a)**

I will count them one by one.

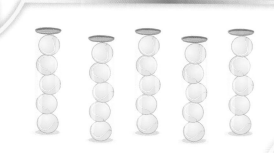

I will count in 5s.

There are 25  in 5 tubes.

**b)**

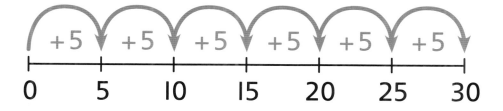

There are 30 in 6 tubes.

I wonder if I have to count again from the beginning?

# Think together

**1** How many  are there in 7 tubes?

| 1 | 2 | 3 | 4 | ⑤ | 6 | 7 | 8 | 9 | ⑩ |
|---|---|---|---|---|---|---|---|---|---|
| 11 | 12 | 13 | 14 | ⑮ | 16 | 17 | 18 | 19 | ⑳ |
| 21 | 22 | 23 | 24 | 25 | 26 | 27 | 28 | 29 | 30 |
| 31 | 32 | 33 | 34 | 35 | 36 | 37 | 38 | 39 | 40 |
| 41 | 42 | 43 | 44 | 45 | 46 | 47 | 48 | 49 | 50 |

0

There are ▢  in 7 tubes.

**2** How many  are there in 8 tubes?

| 1 | 2 | 3 | 4 | 5 | 6 | 7 | 8 | 9 | 10 |
|---|---|---|---|---|---|---|---|---|---|
| 11 | 12 | 13 | 14 | 15 | 16 | 17 | 18 | 19 | 20 |
| 21 | 22 | 23 | 24 | 25 | 26 | 27 | 28 | 29 | 30 |
| 31 | 32 | 33 | 34 | 35 | 36 | 37 | 38 | 39 | 40 |
| 41 | 42 | 43 | 44 | 45 | 46 | 47 | 48 | 49 | 50 |

0

There are ▢ 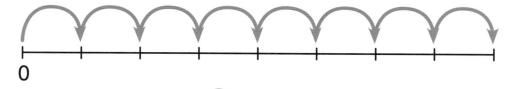 in 8 tubes.

**3** How many  are there in 9 tubes?

How many  are there in 10 tubes?

| 1 | 2 | 3 | 4 | 5 | 6 | 7 | 8 | 9 | 10 |
|---|---|---|---|---|---|---|---|---|---|
| 11 | 12 | 13 | 14 | 15 | 16 | 17 | 18 | 19 | 20 |
| 21 | 22 | 23 | 24 | 25 | 26 | 27 | 28 | 29 | 30 |
| 31 | 32 | 33 | 34 | 35 | 36 | 37 | 38 | 39 | 40 |
| 41 | 42 | 43 | 44 | 45 | 46 | 47 | 48 | 49 | 50 |

0

Would I need to write all the numbers in? I can see a pattern from earlier. I think I know where the numbers go.

107

→ **Practice book 1B p76**

# Solving word problems – addition and subtraction ❶

## Discover

❶ **a)** How many 🍐 did the children pick altogether?

**b)** There were 18 🍐 in the tree.

The children pick their 🍐.

How many 🍐 are left in the tree?

# Share

a)

I need to know how many  each child picked.

I will use ◯ to represent the .

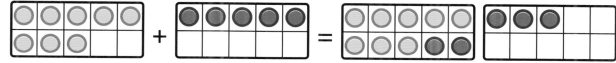

8 + 5 = 13

The children picked 13  altogether.

b)

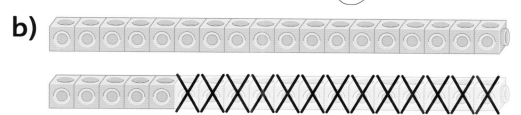

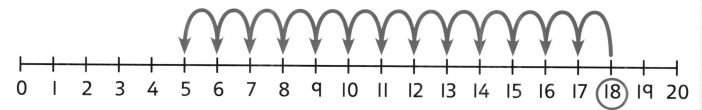

18 − 13 = 5

There are 5  left in the tree.

# Think together

**1** The Scouts are selling 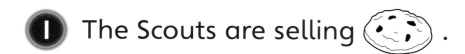.

They have 20 boxes of 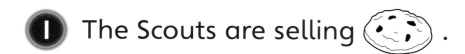.

They sell 5 boxes in the morning.

They sell 9 boxes in the afternoon.

How many boxes do they sell in total?

$5 + 9 = \boxed{\phantom{0}}$

They sell $\boxed{\phantom{0}}$ boxes in total.

**2** There were 20 boxes of 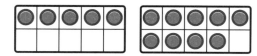 to begin with.

After selling 5 boxes in the morning, how many boxes are left?

$\boxed{\phantom{0}} \bigcirc \boxed{\phantom{0}} = \boxed{\phantom{0}}$

There are $\boxed{\phantom{0}}$ boxes left.

**3** There were 20 boxes of  .

The Scouts sell 5 boxes in the morning and another 9 boxes in the afternoon.

How many boxes are left at the end of the day?

I think I can work it out in two ways.

Can you show the number sentences you used to answer these questions?

III

→ Practice book 1B p79

# Solving word problems – addition and subtraction ②

## Discover

**1** **a)** What can you see in the picture?

Count the different animals.

Share with your partner.

**b)** How many fewer  are in the tree than in the sky?

## Share

I need to sort out the information I can see.

**a)**

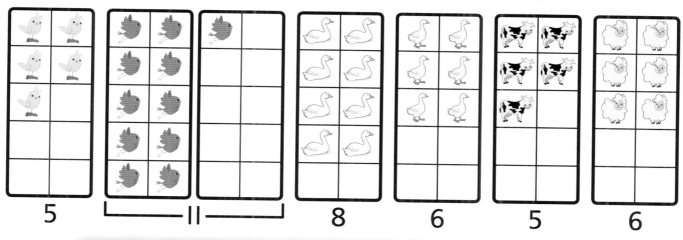

**b)**

I need to find the number of  in the sky and then the number of birds in the tree.

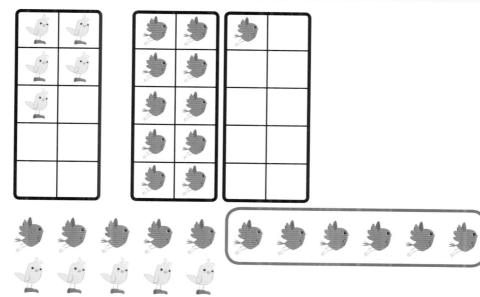

$11 - 5 = 6$

There are 6 fewer birds in the tree than in the sky.

# Think together

**1** **a)** How many more  are in the water than on the bank?

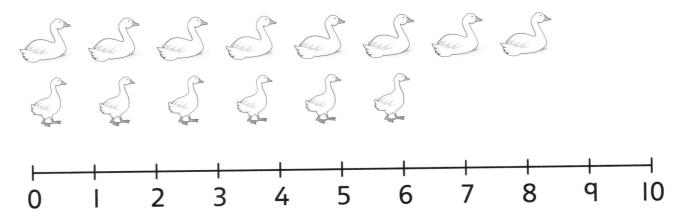

There are ☐ more  in the water than on the bank.

> I wonder if I can make up my own problem using the  ?

**b)** Look again at the picture.

$8 + 6 = $ ☐

What problem does this number sentence solve?

**2** What stories do these number sentences tell?

Talk to a partner.

a)

$8 + 6 = 14$

b)

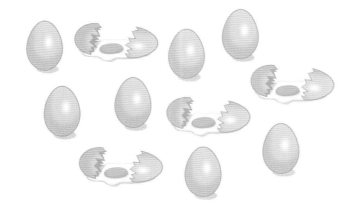

$11 - 4 = 7$

c)

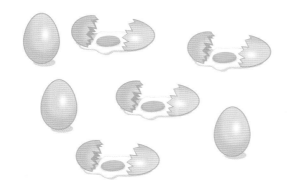

$4 - 3 = 1$

115

→ Practice book 1B p82

# End of unit check

Your teacher will ask you these questions.

**1** What number comes next?

47, 48, 49, ☐

A 410    B 48    C 50    D 15

**2** What is the missing number?

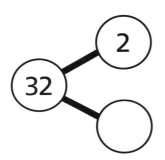

A 3    B 10    C 34    D 30

**3** What is the missing number?

| 45 | 40 | | 30 | 25 |

A 35    B 45    C 39    D 31

**4** Cali has 7 sweets.

Eve has 5 sweets.

How many sweets are there altogether?

Which number sentence **does not** solve the problem?

**A** $12 = 7 + 5$          **C** $7 + 5 = 12$

**B** $7 - 5 = 2$          **D** $5 + 7 = 12$

## Think!

Look at the number. Complete the diagram and answer the questions.

| Make the number using addition | Draw the correct number of objects |
|---|---|
| Complete ☐ < 32 < ☐ | How many tens? ☐ How many ones? ☐ |

**32**

These words might help you.

tens

ones

**part-whole**

**number line**

117

→ **Practice book 1B p85**

# Unit 10
# Introducing length and height

In this unit we will ...
- ⚡ Compare lengths and heights of objects
- ⚡ Use non-standard units to measure objects
- ⚡ Measure with a ruler
- ⚡ Solve word problems about length

We can use cubes to help us compare the length of objects. Which is longer, the pen or the pencil?

We will need some maths words. Can you read them out loud?

**long, longer, longest**

**short, shorter, shortest**

**tall, taller, tallest**

**length     height**

**compare     measure**

We use a ruler to measure lengths. How long is this pencil?

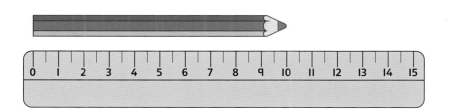

# Comparing lengths and heights

**Discover**

**1 a)** Compare the heights of Anya and Tariq.

Who is **shorter**, who is **taller**?

Look at Jack. How can I see if he is correct?

**b)** Compare the lengths of the three  .

Which is the **longest**?

Which is the **shortest**?

# Share

**a)**

We need to make sure everyone is lined up next to each other.

Anya is shorter than Tariq.

Tariq is taller than Anya.

**b)**

I think the third 〰 is the shortest.

I am not sure. I wonder how we can compare the lengths.

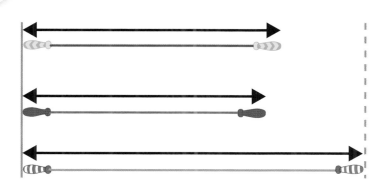

The third 〰 is the longest.

The second 〰 is the shortest.

## Think together

1

Tariq      Anya      Jack

Complete the sentences.

Jack is _____ than Anya.

Tariq is _____ than Anya.

taller

shorter

**2** Complete the sentences.

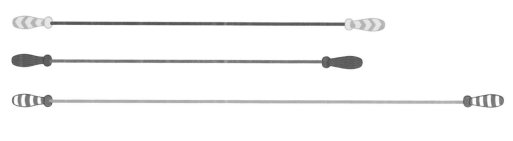

longest

longer

shortest

shorter

The second  is _____

than the first _____ .

The third _____ is the _____

_____ .

**3** How can you compare lengths and heights in your group?

CHALLENGE

How many ways can you order yourselves?

Do we all have to be standing up or sitting down to compare us?

→ **Practice book 1B p87**

# Non-standard units of measure ❶

**Discover**

**❶ a)** Which is longer, the 🚗 or the 🚒 ?

**b)** How many 🧊 long are the 🚗 and

the 🚒 ?

# Share

**a)** The  is longer than the car.

The car is shorter than the fire truck.

**b)**

1  2  3  4  5  6  7  8

1  2  3  4

How do the  show that the fire truck is longer?

The fire truck is 8 🧊 long.

The car is 4 🧊 long.

We need to make sure the 🧊 go from one end to the other.

125

# Think together

**1**

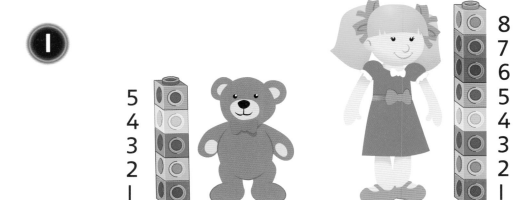

The doll is  tall.

The teddy bear is tall.

The teddy bear is _____ than the doll.

**2**

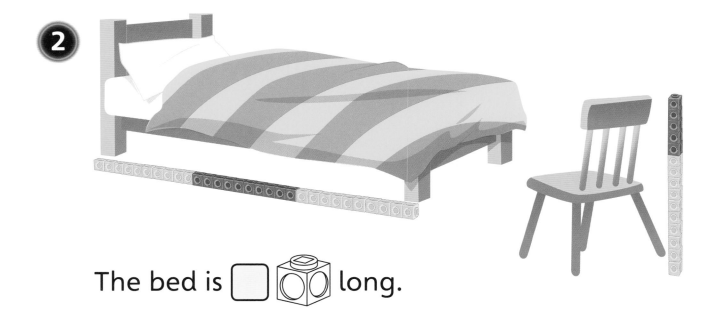

The bed is long.

The chair is tall.

**3** Find objects in the classroom to complete the table.

Say how many  you used to measure each object.

|  | Fewer than 10 cubes | 10 cubes | More than 10 cubes |
|---|---|---|---|
| Tall |  |  |  |
| Long |  |  |  |

Shall I draw then check, or count the  first?

127

→ Practice book 1B p90

# Non-standard units of measure 2

**Discover**

**1  a)** How many ⬜ has the ▱ travelled?

How many 👟 has the ▱ travelled?

**b)** Which is the quicker way to measure the **distance**? Explain your choice.

# Share

**a)**

I am going to count the cubes in 10s.

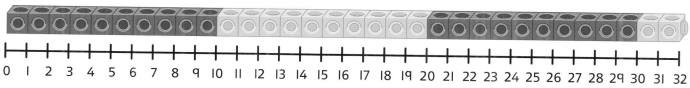

The  has travelled 32 .

If I lose count, how can I check what I have counted?

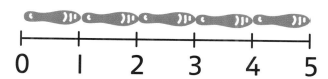

0   1   2   3   4   5

The  has travelled 5 .

**b)** Counting with  is quicker because you do not have to lay out lots of .

Is there anything else we could have used?

# Think together

**a)** Would you measure the length of the field with

 or  ?

**b)** What would you use to measure the length of a

 ?

**2** What would you use to measure the following?

a) The height of a door  or

b) The length of a table  or

c) The length of your shoe  or

**3** How long is your classroom?

CHALLENGE

| Unit of measure | How many units? |
|---|---|
| book | |
| | |
| | |

I wonder why the amount of units changes.

131

→ Practice book 1B p93

# Measuring length using a ruler

**Discover**

Both pieces of string are 4 cubes long.

**1** **a)** Which is the longer piece of string?

Explain how both pieces of string can be

4 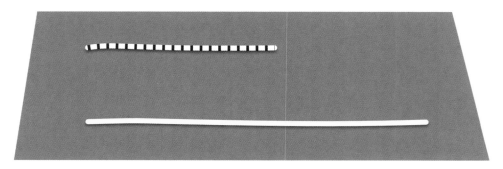 long.

**b)** Use a **ruler** to measure both pieces of string.

# Share

**a)** 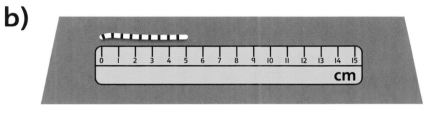 is longer.

They are both 4 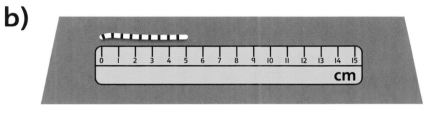 long but the 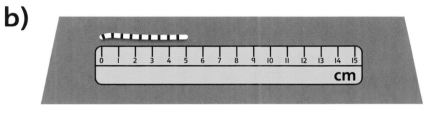 are different sizes.

**b)**

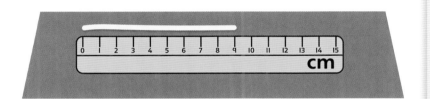 is 5 cm long.

is 9 cm long.

cm stands for **centimetre**. These rulers are not real rulers so the centimetres are not quite the correct length. A real centimetre is about the size of your thumb.

cm

All real cm are exactly the same.

# Think together

**1**

How long is the string?

The string is ⬜ cm.

**2** Use this ruler to measure a small pencil.

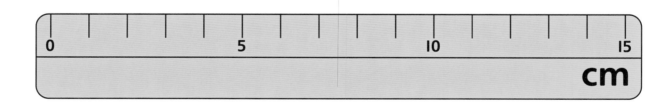

This ruler is the same size as a real ruler.

Measure your partner's pencil. Is your pencil longer or shorter than your partner's pencil?

**3** Find three objects you could draw in each box. Use a ruler to measure them.

CHALLENGE

| Shorter than 10 cm | 10 cm or longer | 10 cm or taller |
|---|---|---|
|  |  |  |

I found a rubber. It is 7 cm long. I will draw this in the first box.

My pencil case is 10 cm tall. Can I draw it in any box?

135

→ **Practice book 1B p96**

# Solving word problems – length

## Discover

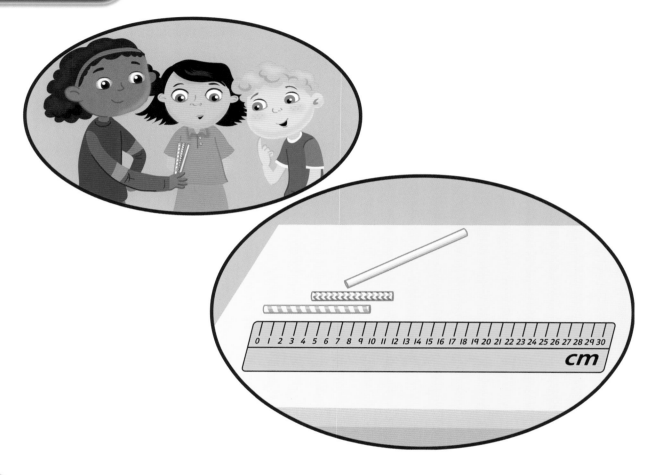

**I** **a)** Work out the length of 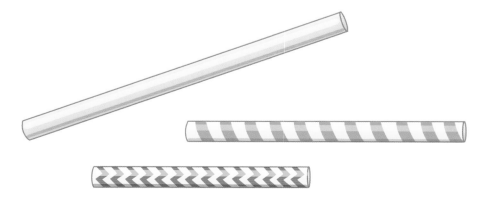 .

**b)** Order all the straws from shortest to longest.

# Share

I did 11 − 4 = 7.

**a)**

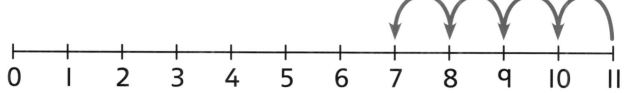

I moved the straw to start at zero.

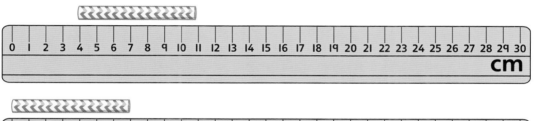

The length of  is 7 cm.

**b)**

I can work out two from the picture.

I think I will need to move one of the straws to measure it correctly.

shortest
↓
longest

# Think together

**1** Kiko puts 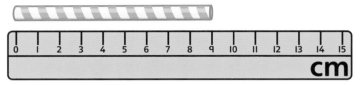 and  next to each other in a line.

What is the total length?

The length of straw 1 is ☐ .

The length of straw 2 is ☐ .

☐ + ☐ = ☐

The total length is ☐ cm.

**2** Which train is 3 cm tall?

I wonder why they are not both 3 cm.

138

**3** What is the difference in length between the 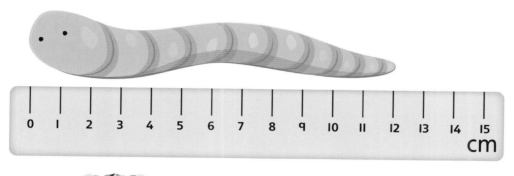 and the 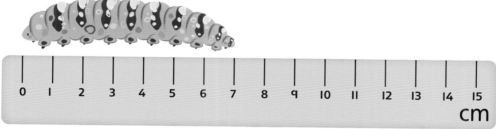 ?

CHALLENGE

The difference in length is ☐ cm.

I think I need to do a subtraction for this question.

I am just going to count on.

→ Practice book 1B p99

# End of unit check

Your teacher will ask you these questions.

**1** Which statement is false?

**A** The 🐻 is taller than the 🐯 .

**B** The 🐯 is the shortest.

**C** The 🦒 is shorter than the 🐻 .

**D** The 🦒 is the tallest.

**2** Which image shows the  is 5 ⬜ long?

**A**

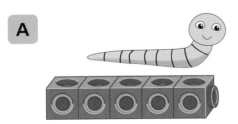

**B**

**C**

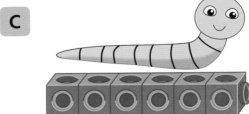

**D**

**3** How tall is the mug?

Use a ruler.

A 4 cm    B 2 cm    C 3 cm    D 5 cm

**4** How long is the piece of rock?

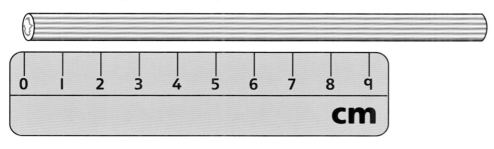

A 9 cm    B 12 cm    C 3 cm    D 18 cm

## Think!

Which piece of string is longer? Explain your choice.

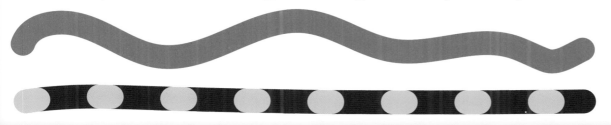

These words might help you.

longer    shorter

curved    straight

141

→ Practice book 1B p102

# Unit 11
# Introducing weight and volume

In this unit we will …
- ⚡ Compare the weight of objects
- ⚡ Weigh objects
- ⚡ Compare the capacity of objects
- ⚡ Measure capacity
- ⚡ Solve word problems about weight and capacity

Have you seen one of these before? It is a balance scale. We can use it to compare the weight of objects. Which item do you think is heavier?

We will need some maths words. Can you read them out loud?

**heavier, heaviest**     **lighter, lightest**

**capacity**          **balance scales**

**full**     **empty**     **compare**

**weight, weigh**     **balanced**

**measure**     **estimate**

We can use glasses to measure capacity. Which jug had the most squash in it?

# Comparing weight

**Discover**

Put the heavier one in the bag first.

James

**1** **a)** James has a 🍍 and a 🍎.

Which is **heavier**?

**b)** Which is **lighter**, 🥛 or 🧴?

## Share

I think the  feels heavier.

**a)**

I used **balance scales** to compare the objects.

 is down and  is up.

 is heavier than  .

 is lighter than  .

You can use < to mean lighter than and > to mean heavier than.

 <

 >

**b)**

 is up and  is down.

 is lighter than  .

# Think together

**1** Which is heavier? Which is lighter?

 is _____ than ⬤ .

⬤ is _____ than 🥣 .

**2** Which items are lighter than  ? Which items are heavier?

One scale is **balanced**. I can't see which item is heavier!

**3** Who is correct?

CHALLENGE

Sam

The balloon will go down because it is bigger.

Katie

They will be equal because they are the same shape.

Maria

The balloon will go up because it is lighter.

Hassan

The egg will go down because it is lighter.

I think the bigger items are heavier.

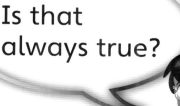

Is that always true?

147

→ Practice book 1B p104

# Measuring weight

**Discover**

Hiro    Lucy    Joe

**1** **a)** Hiro places one more .

Now the book balances the 10 .

My book balances 10 cubes.

My book balances 5 cubes.

Who is correct?

**b)** Why does Lucy need fewer cubes than Hiro?

# Share

**a)** There were 9  .

Hiro adds one more  .

The book balances 10  .

> I know Joe is wrong.
> You cannot measure if the cubes are different sizes.

Hiro is correct.

**b)** Lucy uses different cubes to **weigh** the book.

 are heavier than  .

Lucy uses heavier cubes, so she does not need as many to balance the book.

# Think together

**1** Record the **weight** of the .

 weighs ☐ .

 weighs ☐ .

 weighs ☐ ◯.

Why does the trainer balance more ◯ than ☐ ?

**2** Copy and complete the table.

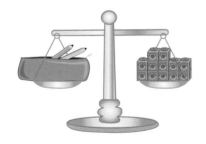 

| Object | Weight in 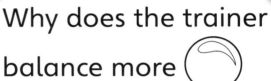 |
|---|---|
| ✏ | |
| | 12 |
| ⬛ | |
| | 1 |

**3**

## How could you balance the scales?

I can find more than one way.

I know how many balance one book. This is a book and I more.

→ Practice book 1B p107

# Comparing weight using measuring

**Discover**

Heaviest items on bottom shelf. Lightest items on top shelf.

Sale!

**1** **a)** Which box goes on the top shelf?

Which box goes on the bottom shelf?

**b)** Put the boxes in order from **heaviest** to **lightest**.

Use ☐ > ☐ > ☐ to show this.

## Share

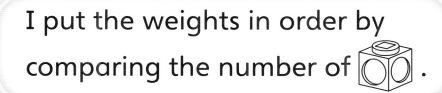

I put the weights in order by comparing the number of .

a)

I remember how to put numbers in order.

 weighs 10 .  weighs 13 .

10        <        13

   <  

    <   

 is heavier than .

 weighs less than 10 . So  weighs

less than .

 is the heaviest. It goes on the bottom shelf.

 is the lightest. It goes on the top shelf.

b)   >  > 

153

# Think together

**1**

Complete the sentences.

**a)** 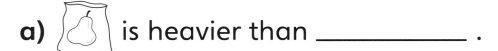 is heavier than _____ .

**b)**  is _____ than  .

**c)** 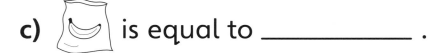 is equal to _____ .

> Heaviest items on bottom. Lightest items on top.

**2**

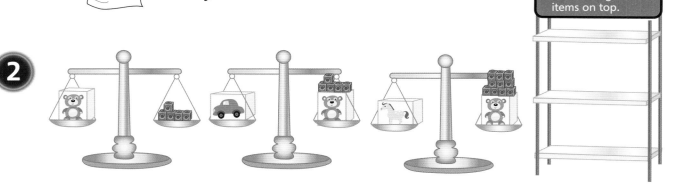

Work out the correct shelf for each box.

The _____ box goes on the bottom.

The _____ box goes in the middle.

The _____ box goes on the top.

☐ > ☐ > ☐

**3** How many  could the and the each weigh?

CHALLENGE

Can you see more than one possible answer?

155

# Comparing capacity

**Discover**

**I** **a)** Which of these does Molly want?

**b)** Which  is **full?**

Which is **empty?**

# Share

**a)**

> I compared the glasses by looking for the level of squash.

Molly wants less than  .

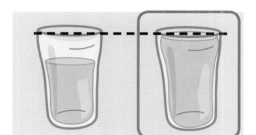

This glass has more than  .

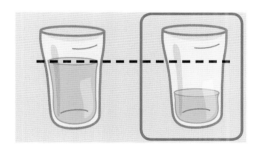

This glass has less than  .

Molly wants this glass.

**b)**

This glass is full.      This glass is empty.

# Think together

1 Put these in order, from empty to full.

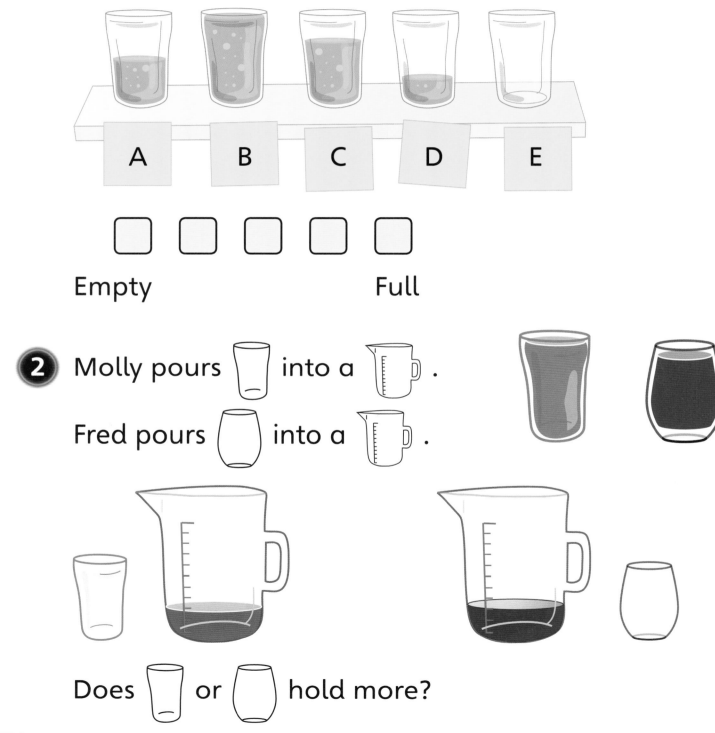

A     B     C     D     E

□ □ □ □ □

Empty                    Full

2 Molly pours ☐ into a ☐ .

Fred pours ☐ into a ☐ .

Does ☐ or ☐ hold more?

**3**

CHALLENGE

 I would like an ice cube, please.

 I would like a full glass of juice, please.

I would like more than a half full glass of juice, please.

 Fred

 Molly

 Sam

## Which drinks could each person have?

I think there is more than one answer.

I wonder if there are any drinks that no one wants.

159

# Measuring capacity

**Discover**

I used 20 🥄 to fill the bucket.

Mr Chabra

Fred

Ava

**1  a)** Circle the correct answer to complete the sentences.

10 🥄 / 🥤 filled the bucket.

3 🥄 / 🥤 filled the bucket.

**b)** Mr Chabra estimates that it will take 3 🥄 to fill the bucket.

Ava estimates 12 🥄. Fred estimates 6 🥄.

Who is correct?

# Share

Capacity means how much a container can hold.

a)

20 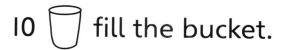 fill the bucket.

10 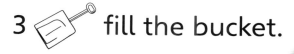 fill the bucket.

3  fill the bucket.

We can say the bucket has a capacity of 10  .

So, the bucket has a capacity of 3 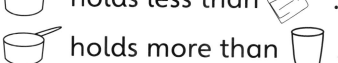 .

b) 🥄 holds less than 🥄 .

🥄 holds more than 🥛 .

Mr Chabra estimates 3 🥄 to fill the bucket, but that is too few.

Ava estimates 12 🥄 , but that is too many.

Fred is correct.

# Think together

**1** Two children helped each other to fill the bucket.

How many  fill the bucket?

I put in 4 🥄.

I put in 5 🥄.

☐ + ☐ = ☐

☐ 🥄 fill the bucket.

**2** Complete the table.

| Container | How many needed to fill 🍚 |
|---|---|
| 🥣 | |
| | 15 |
| 🥤 | |

**3** Who is right?

This jug holds 6 glasses.

Mr Chabra

This jug holds 8 glasses.

Mrs Hodge

This jug holds 5 glasses.

Mrs Shaw

→ Practice book 1B p116

# Comparing capacity using measuring

**Discover**

**1  a)** Complete the sentences.

| A | B | C | D |

☐ is filled by 2 cups.  ☐ is filled by 15 cups.

☐ is filled by 5 cups.  ☐ is filled by 15 cups.

**b)** Put the containers in order of capacity, from greatest to smallest.

# Share

**a)**

I know that 15 > 5 > 2, so the largest container is filled by 15 cups.

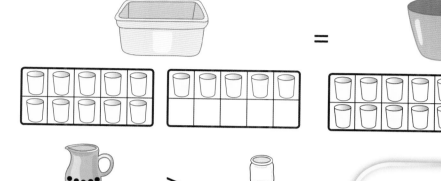

=

 >

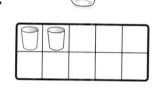

The two large containers must each have a capacity of 15 cups.

5 > 2

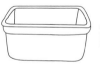 is filled by 5 cups.

is filled by 2 cups.

is filled by 15 cups.

is filled by 15 cups.

**b)**

greatest    smallest

# Think together

**1** Match the buckets to the cups.

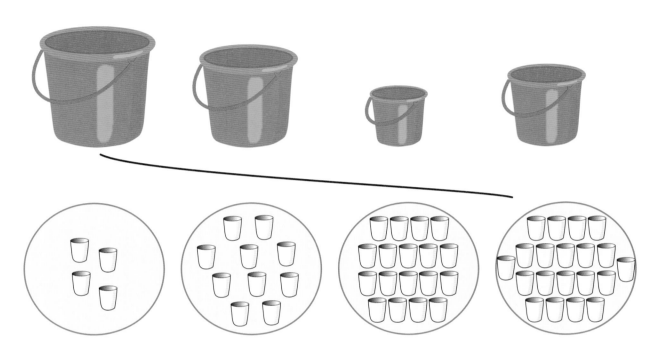

**2** Complete the sentences using <, > or =.

| Container | Fills |
|---|---|
| | □□□ |
| | □□□□□ □□ |
| | □□□□□ |

**3** Use A, B and C to complete the sentences.

CHALLENGE

A

B

C

There is still some water in Jug B, but the glasses are all full.

Jug ⬜ > Jug ⬜ > Jug ⬜

Jug ⬜ < Jug ⬜ < Jug ⬜

167

→ Practice book 1B p119

# Solving word problems – weight and capacity

## Discover

The jug holds 10 glasses.

The pan holds 6 glasses.

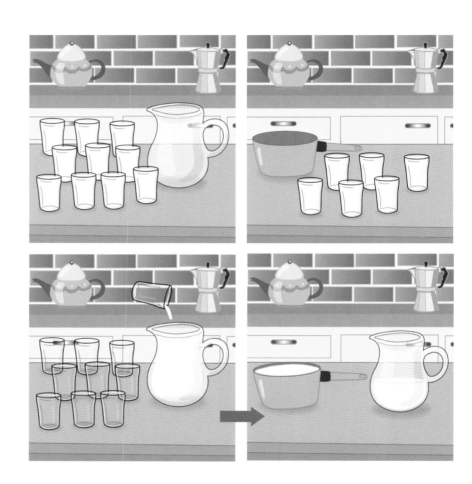

**1 a)** How many  are there left in the jug?

**b)** How many  will there be in the ?

# Share

**a)**

I know that there were 10  in the jug when we started. Then some was poured out.

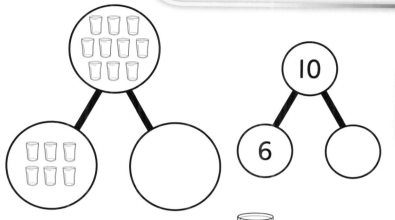

This is a subtraction. I will break the whole into two parts.

There were 10  in the jug.

6 glasses fill the .

10 − 6 = 4

There are 4  left in the jug.

**b)**

10  in the jug.

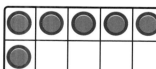

6 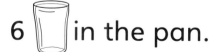 in the pan.

10 + 6 = 16

There will be 16  in the .

# Think together

**1** How many cups of rice will be in the pan?

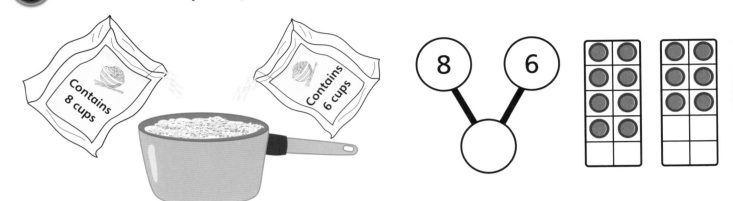

There are ⬜ cups of rice in the pan.

**2** How much does a small ⬛ weigh?

A small ⬜ weighs the same as ⬜ ⬛ .

**3** **a)**

How many  balance 1  ?

I used 1 cube to represent the weight of 1  Then I worked out how many cubes represented 1  .

**b)**

How many  balance 1  ?

→ Practice book 1B p122

# End of unit check

Your teacher will ask you these questions.

**1** Which is true?

**A**  is heavier than △ .

**B** weighs the same as △ .

**C** △ is lighter than ☐ .

**D** △ is heavier than ☐ .

**2** Which ☐ do we know weighs 8 ☐ ?

**A**          **B**          **C**          **D**

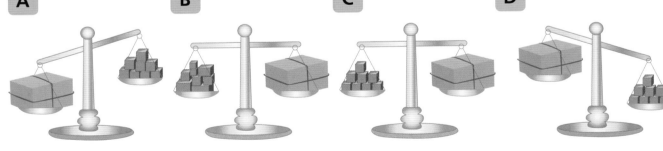

**3** Which jug has more than  ?

**A**          **B**          **C**          **D**

**4** How many  balance one ⬚ ?

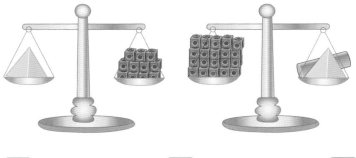

**A** 20      **B** 11      **C** 1      **D** 9

## Think!

How much would 10 glasses of water weigh?
Give the number of blocks.

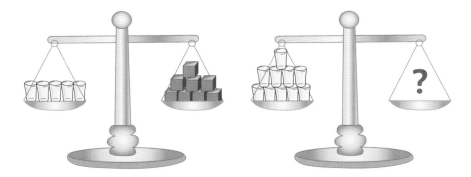

I know that 10 glasses of water would weigh ⬚ blocks because ...

These words might help you.

lighter      heavier

more      fewer

→ Practice book 1B p125

# What do we know now?

Can you do all these things?

⚡ Add numbers within 20
⚡ Subtract numbers within 20
⚡ Work with numbers up to 50
⚡ Measure and compare length and height
⚡ Measure and compare weight and volume

It's ok to get things wrong. It helps us learn!

Now you're ready for the next books!

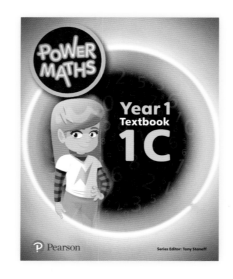